I0623305

SHOULD WAR BE ELIMINATED?

Philosophical and Theological Investigations

The 1984 Père Marquette
Theology Lecture

SHOULD WAR
BE ELIMINATED?

Philosophical and Theological
Investigations

by

STANLEY HAUERWAS

Professor of Theology
Notre Dame University

MARQUETTE UNIVERSITY PRESS
MILWAUKEE, WISCONSIN 53233

BT
736.2
- H34
1984

Library of Congress Catalogue Card Number: 84-060236

ISBN 0-87462-539-4

Preface

The 1984 Père Marquette Lecture is the fifteenth in a series inaugurated to celebrate the Tercentenary of the missions and explorations of Père Marquette, S.J. (1637-1675). The Marquette University Theology Department, founded in 1952, launched these annual lectures by distinguished theologians under the title of the Père Marquette Lectures in 1969.

The 1984 lecture was delivered at Marquette University April 8, 1984 by Dr. Stanley Hauerwas, professor of theology at Notre Dame University.

Dr. Hauerwas received his Ph.D. in religious ethics from Yale University in 1968. He has published *Vision and Virtue: Essays in Theological Ethics* (1974), *Character and Christian Life: A Study In Theological Ethics* (1975), *Truthfulness and Tragedy: Further Investigations,* (1977), and a *Community of Character: Towards a Constructive Social Ethics* (1981).

His lectures and articles – e.g. "The Church in a Divided World: the Interpretive Power of the Christian Story", "The Moral Authority of Scripture: the Politics and Ethics and Remembering" – concern Christian ethics in the modern world. He insists on the radicality of the gospel message and its conflict with certain moral theories and practices.

Dr. Hauerwas has recently published *The Peaceable Kingdom: A Primer in Christian Ethics* in 1984, and is preparing a book on war and other related topics called *Living Among the Nations: Reflections on War, Democracy and Survival.*

Should War Be Eliminated?: Philosophical and Theological Investigations

> Cain said to Abel his brother, "Let us go out to the field." And when they were in the field, Cain rose up against his brother Abel, and killed him. Then the Lord said to Cain, "Where is Abel your brother?" He said, "I do not know; am I my brother's keeper?"

And so it began.

1. On Getting the Problems Right

Large numbers of people are now convinced that we should eliminate all nuclear weapons. In their recent pastoral letter the Roman Catholic Bishops of America seem virtually to have joined these ranks. Still more people, while they do not call for the complete destruction of nuclear weapons suggest that we should drastically reduce the kind and number of our nuclear stockpile. This latter group includes such highly respected persons as George Kennan and Robert MacNamara, the sort who cannot be accused of political naïveté. As yet, however, these many voices have precipitated no change in public policy and they seem unlikely to do so in the near future. Indeed we are told that the peace movement threatens the peace, as peace can only be guaranteed through strength which means more, not less, nuclear missiles. And so the stockpiles continue to grow.

Why do we seem caught in this dilemma? Why, when all admit that nuclear weapons threaten our very existence as nations if not as a species, do we seem so unable to free ourselves from their power? Some suppose the people want peace, but our leaders, inspired by some nefarious motive, do not. Such explanations are far too simple; the problem is much more recalcitrant than a change in leadership can solve. We all, leaders and followers alike, seem caught in a web of powers that is one of our own making yet not under our control. We say we want peace, but we seem destined for war.

Why is this the case? Why do all our attempts to think morally about war seem often so futile in the face of war's irresistible inevitability? In spite of its horror and destructiveness, its insanity and irrationality, might it be that we have overlooked the fact that war has a moral purpose? Could that be the reason why no matter how compelling the logic against nuclear weapons, we still seem defeated by those who say, "All that may be quite right, but. . .?" What are the moral presuppositions that make that "but" seem so powerful?

In order to try to understand these kinds of questions I am going to propose a thought experiment which may help us reconsider our assumptions about war and its place in our lives. The experiment is to provide the best negative answer I am able to the question: "Should war be eliminated?" We tend to think such a question absurd. After all, it is not a question of "should" at all, but "can." We all know we should eliminate war; the problem is we cannot. Asking if we should eliminate war is like asking if we should eliminate sin. Of course we should, but the problem is that we cannot. Therefore to ask such a question is to start us off in the wrong direction.

While admitting that there may be aspects of the question bordering on the absurd, I hope to show that by pressing it seriously we may be able to illumine why war is such an intractable aspect of our existence. Moreover, by insisting on using the language of "should" I want to force us to consider what is at stake morally by the very fact we describe some forms of violence as war. Too often those concerned to make moral judgments about war, whether they be pacifist or just-war theorist, assume that the description "war" is unproblematic – the only question is how to eliminate or control war. Yet that is exactly what I am suggesting cannot be assumed.

It may be objected that just-war theory in fact does presuppose the kind of analysis of war I am suggesting. Rather than being a theory about the criteria necessary to determine if or how a war may be fought morally, the just-war is an attempt to understand war as a moral enterprise. I have no reason to deny such an interpretation of the just-war. Moreover, if in fact that is what just-war theory is about, then the moral description of war I will try to develop can be seen as an attempt to make candid implicit assumptions entailed by just-war thinking.

Ethical reflection about war, therefore, does not begin by asking what makes a war more or less just. Rather a morality is already implied by the very fact we call it war. For war is not simply another name for violence.

We must begin, therefore, by asking: Do we know what we mean by calling something a war? Certainly war entails violence, but yet the very description "war" seems to propose a different moral evaluation than violence. At the very least "war" denotes purposive human activity which "violence" does not always imply. Perhaps that is why normal categories dealing with killing do not seem to apply in war. For example, we are taken aback by the suggestion that war is but legitimized murder on a mass scale. Our resistance to calling war murder indicates we assume it has a moral legitimacy, or at least it is not morally illegitimate as is murder.

Indeed some who currently argue against nuclear weapons do so in defense of war as an important moral institution. From their perspective war is being ruined by modern weapons of mass destruction. They deny that "nuclear war" is appropriately so called because war presupposes that good can be done through its prosecution. Thus George Kennan challenges "the thesis that these devices, the so called nuclear weapons, are really weapons at all – that they deserve that designation. A weapon is something with which you try to affect the purposes and the concepts of an opponent; it is not something with which you blindly destroy his entire civilization, and probably your own as well."[1] We might say that Kennan, and others who argue like him, are trying to eliminate nuclear war in order to make the world safe for war. But we must ask if their position is coherent, for once the moral presuppositions underlying their acceptance of war are made candid, it may be the case that nuclear weapons are but a new development in the institution of war.

If it is so important to save war as a significant moral option, we need an account that makes explicit war's moral status. In spite of all calls for peace, such an account might show us that if war were eliminated we would be morally the worse for it. By this I do not mean merely that we would miss the extraordinary individual heroics often associated with war, or lose the kind of comradeship war creates between soldiers and citizens.[2] It is undoubtedly true that war often provides the occasion for our most impressive moral behavior, but these good results are not contained within the very fabric of war itself. The issue is not whether war occasionally can have good results, but whether war, with all its horror, destructiveness, and brutality, is an institution that nonetheless serves moral purposes which we should not will to be without.

This is the issue I seek to address although I honestly must say I am skeptical if any response can be coherent. In particular I fear any abstract account of "war" risks lapsing into a false idealism. What we need to talk about is not war, but this or that war. Philosophical analysis of the kind I propose has the dangerous tendency to console by offering explanations for what is essentially inexplicable.

So why pursue it? First I hope by proceeding in this manner we will be able to get beyond some of the current rhetoric about nuclear war and deal with the basic issue of war itself. The current debate about nuclear weapons in a disturbing fashion is beginning to resemble the conflict over abortion. Both sides have arguments and responses to which the opponent does not listen. By directing our attention to war rather than simply the morality of nuclear weapons, I hope to raise new questions which will perhaps prevent our discussion from ending in a shouting match. I do not intend to solve the moral problems raised by nuclear deterrence strategy; rather my purpose is to try to help us understand morally how we have arrived in a situation where our so-called safety can be insured only if we are willing to will countless deaths and destruction. I want first to understand, not judge or offer solutions.

Secondly, by developing a moral case for war I hope to illumine the ambivalence Christians often exhibit about war. That ambivalence is at the heart of *The Challenge of Peace: God's Promise and Our Response.*[3] The kind of ambivalence with which I am concerned is not the bishops' unwillingness to condemn forthrightly all forms of deterrence. Rather I wish to call our attention to the even more fundamental ambivalence concerning war itself. For in spite of the bishops' avowal that Christians are fundamentally a people of peace, they affirm that Christians can participate in war as a legitimate moral endeavor. I hope to show, in spite of the bishops' assertion that war is always the result of sin (a fact they continue to presume, and it is a presumption consistent with the natural law basis of the just-war tradition) that war is a morally positive institution.

Finally I want to develop as strong a case as I can for war because I am a pacifist. Too often pacifists try to win easy victories against those who support war by stressing war's irrationality and horror. The problem with such strategy is, in spite of war's obvious irrationalities and horrors, it somehow is beside the point. It is so, I think, because it ignores the powerful moral presupposition that sustains war's viability in spite of its brutality. The significance of the pacifist's refusal to cooperate with war can only be appreciated by understanding why war has such a hold on our moral imagination.

Moreover, by proceeding in this way I hope we will also be able to better understand the theological disagreements between pacifist and just-war thinkers.[4] For by developing a positive case for war I hope to show that pacifist and just-war thinkers draw on quite different assumptions about eschatology. Both entail assumptions about how history should be told and the Christian role in it. By suggesting how war determines our history we can better understand why Christians cannot allow that history to define their existence. Pacifism, therefore, is not just an attitude about war, but it entails the belief that God, through Jesus Christ, has inaugurated a history that frees all people from our assumption that we have no moral alternative to war.

2. War in a Catholic Perspective

The suggestion that Christians have a moral ambivalence about war leads us to suppose that some explicit theological justification of war might be at work as well as the more generally accepted moral ones. Investigation of two significant documents: John XXIII's, *Pacem in Terris* and the recent Pastoral Letter of the American Roman Catholic Bishops, *The Challenge of Peace: God's Promise and Our Response* show this to be the case. In the following treatment of them it is not my intention to try to give a complete analysis, but rather to try to make explicit each document's understanding of war. For though each says much about the ethics of war neither tries to explain what they understand war to be. By attending to how they make their ethical case I hope to show that their implicit understanding of war is more positive than their ethical prouncements about war would lead one to believe.

I have chosen these documents because they are representative of a church's position rather than that of an individual thinker. Moreover they bring to bear elements, some conflictual, from a Christian tradition that has

developed the most sophisticated moral analysis of war. While documents urge peace, they
nonetheless continue to maintain war as a
moral possibility, if not a duty, for Christians.
I hope my criticism of these documents will
expose these assumptions as well as generate
some of the conceptual tools we will need to
understand war in a more positive light.

Pacem in Terris was promulgated in 1963
and brought a new emphasis on peace by a
church that had in the past generally been
associated with the just-war tradition. [5] In
Pacem in Terris the just-war theory is subor-
dinated to a wider vision of peace. Thus John
XXIII argues, "There will never be peace
among men unless peace resides in the soul
of each man: – unless each person preserves
within himself the order commanded by God"
(165). That order is to be found in the natural
law which can be known by all people. It's
most basic principle is "that every human
being is a person naturally endowed with
intelligence and free will. Thus man has rights
and duties flowing directly and conjointly
from his very nature. These rights and duties
are universal and inviolable and therefore
inalienable" (9).

Every human right, the right of life, truth,

conscience, family, work, private property,
assembly, political participation, is connected
with a corresponding set of duties. Since we
are social by nature a well ordered society is
one where "every natural right of a man and
the duties of others to acknowledge and foster
that right is recognized" (30). In such a society
authority is primarily a moral force as order
is maintained by an "appeal primarily to the
conscience of individual citizens: – to the duty
of each one to work willingly for the common
good of all. Since all men are naturally equal
in human dignity, no one has the power to
force compliance on another, except God
alone, Who sees and judges the unseen
thoughts of men's hearts" (48).

Thus the encyclical assumes an organic
view of society where each nation contains
elements of the common good by safeguard-
ing the personal rights and duties of individuals (60). Society, and the state which serves
it, is peaceful since by definition it seems
there can be no conflict between rights if
everyone is allowed to pursue those rights
fairly. The more we cooperate the less we will
need to resort to violence.

This basic assumption is then applied to international affairs. Each state has "reciprocal

rights and duties and the relations between States should be harmonized in truth, justice, active cooperation, and liberty. For the same natural law which governs the relations between individual men must also regulate those between states" (80). Thus the relations between States must be governed by truth. Truth calls for the elimination of every form of racism and recognition of the inviolable and immutable principle that all states are by nature equal in dignity. Each state therefore has the right to exist, to make progress, to possess the means for its development, and to bear the principal responsibility for bringing about and expanding its own progress and growth. Truth also demands that each nation have the right to its good name and to due honor" (86).

It may be that the advantages each state seeks to acquire will lead to disagreements but these should be settled not by force of arms but by "appraisal of the arguments and attitudes of the opposing sides, a mature and objective weighing of the facts, and an equitable adjustment of the opposing views" (93). Peace, therefore, cannot be based on the stockpiling of weapons, but on mutual trust. "Justice, right reason, and an appreciation of

the dignity of man urgently demand that the
arms race stop; that weapons on hand in the
various countries be reduced through parallel
and simultaneous action by the parties concerned; that nuclear weapons be banned; and
that all men finally come to an agreement on
a suitable disarmament program with an
effective system for mutual control" (112).

It is easy to accuse *Pacem in Terris* of
naïveté, but I think such an accusation over-
looks the substantive assumptions embodied
in the Encyclical. These assumptions are all
the more powerful because they are widely
shared. Like the Encyclical, many assume
that war is the result of a failure to give persons their rights to pursue their interests. If
each of us is satisfied in himself we would be
at peace with one another; in like manner
nation states would be at peace having nothing to gain by aggression. War is not so much
wrong, therefore, as it is plain irrational.

Yet the view that peace results from cooperation between free individuals is seriously
flawed. Flawed not because we are more
fundamentally depraved than the Encyclical
assumes, though I certainly think it is far too
optimistic concerning human good will, but
because the kind of violence embodied in the

institution of war is not due to the pursuit of our interests at the expense of others but rather, as I hope to show, results from our moral commitment to the good of others. That the Encyclical fails to confront this reality of war causes, I think, its calls for peace to appear flaccid. We thus dismiss it as but another idealistic call for peace in a world constituted by war.

Pacem in Terris, however, is not only a vision peculiar to the Catholic church, but it also articulates a view of peace that is the working assumption of many schooled by the Enlightenment. It may seem odd to suggest that the Catholic church, the great enemy of the Enlightenment, has now become its most prominent advocate, but I think that is what has happened. For the working assumption of the Encyclical is something like this: There is a fundamental symmetry between establishing and maintaining a just constitution within a state and in establishing and maintaining a just relationship between states.[6] If we could instruct just states of autonomous moral agents then we could secure peace between them, reserving war only for protection against unjust aggressor states.

The Challenge of Peace begins by asserting,

quite contrary to these Enlightenment assumptions, that the Christians' longing for
peace is based in the Gospel rather than
natural law. The bishops suggest that there
can be no question that Jesus was on the side
of peace against war.[7] Indeed Jesus not only
taught peace but, as the full demonstration
of the power of God's reign made present in
his life and work, Jesus gives a peace beyond
what is possible for relations between autonomous nation states (51). "Jesus gives that
peace to his disciples, to those who had wit-
nessed the helplessness of the crucifixion and
the power of the resurrection (Jn. 20:19, 20,
26). The peace which he gives to them as he
greets them as their risen Lord is the fullness
of salvation. It is the reconciliation of the
world and God (Rom. 5:1-2; Col. 1:20); the
restoration of the unity and harmony of all
creation which the Old Testament spoke of
with such longing. Because the walls of hostil-
ity between God and humankind were broken
down in the life and death of the true, perfect
servant, union and well-being between God
and the world were finally fully possible (Eph.
2:13-22; Gal. 3:28)" (51).

Nevertheless, the bishops go on to say, the
peace and reconciliation Jesus left with the

early Christians "were not yet fully operative in their world" (53). They assert on the one hand that "Jesus Christ is our peace, and in his death-resurrection he gives God's peace to our world," (54) but on the other hand, it is false to suppose that Jesus or the scriptures provide us with a "detailed answer to the specifics of the questions which we face today. They do not speak specifically of nuclear war or nuclear weapons, for these were beyond the imagination of the communities in which the scriptures were formed. The sacred texts do, however, provide us with urgent direction when we look at today's concrete realities. The fullness of eschatological peace remains before us in hope and yet the gift of peace is already ours in the reconciliation effected in Jesus Christ" (55).[8]

Thus the Christian must live between the vision of the reign of God and its concrete realization in history. Any ethical response to war must be worked out in the light of this tension. Christians may take different stances about war as they move toward the realization of God's kingdom in history, but all Christians will "find in any violent situation the consequences of sin: not only sinful patterns of domination, oppression or aggression, but the conflict of values and interests which illustrate the limitations of a sinful world" (61). Therefore pacifism is a legitimate response by Christians to war, but it is not that which the bishops take. For while their letter is addressed "principally to the Catholic community, we want it to make a contribution to the wider public debate in our country on the dangers and dilemmas of the nuclear age"[9]. Therefore the ethical basis of the Pastoral must be one that is not based on specifically Christian presuppositions.

In order to develop a position capable of providing such guidance the bishops, in spite of their analysis of the New Testament, turn to the just-war theory. That theory they argue is built on the fundamental assumption that "governments threatened by armed, unjust aggression must defend their people. This includes defense by armed force if necessary as a last resort" (75). We therefore have a "fundamental right of defense." Even more strongly put, the bishops quote Pius XII who argued that "A people threatened with an unjust aggression, or already its victim, may not remain passively indifferent, if it would think and act as befits a Christian. Their defense is even an obligation for the nations as a whole, who have a duty not to abandon a nation that is attacked" (76).

Thus while recommending non-violent means to fend off aggression, the bishops candidly suggest "we must recognize the reality of the paradox we face as Christians living in the context of the world as it presently exists; we must continue to articulate our belief that love is possible and the only real hope for all human relations, and yet accept that force, even deadly force, is sometimes justified and that nations must provide for their defense" (78).[10] For it is an essential presupposition of Catholic teaching about war that "every nation has a right and duty to defend itself against unjust aggression" (p. iii).

For my purposes it is not necessary to pursue the bishops' detailed account of the just war theory, its implications for nuclear weapons, and their arguments against deterrence. The crucial issues have alrealy been joined by their willingness to underwrite the presumption that the state has the right and duty to defend itself and yet maintain that, in principle, peace should be possible in our world. Once the former presumption has been granted, and it is not clear why they grant it, it is not easy to see how what they say

about the Gospel's commitment to peace can
be anything more than an unrealizable ideal.

Of course it may be asked what is wrong
about having such an ideal. Given the fact that
we live in a war-ridden world, it would seem
to be a good idea at least to keep the goal of
peace ever before us. But I am not so sure
that is the case. For such an ideal might well
encourage us, if war is not only a necessary
but morally necessary part of our lives, to self-
deceptive explanations for our involvement
with war. It may well be war is "the result
of sin and a tragic remedy for sin in the life
of political societies," but even as such war
can serve moral purposes.

Perhaps what we need to learn from this
is that, while it sounds right to say war is due
to sin, such claims are of little interest. For
such a description does not help us understand what war is and why it seems such an
inevitable part of our lives. Therefore I will
try to give an account of war that goes beyond
such broad categories in the hope that by it
we will better understand why the bishops
cannot bring themselves to deny war as an
institution integral to the nation state.

For there seem to be two different views
of war in *The Challenge of Peace* that reflect

the two different ethical perspectives of the Pastoral – the one based on the Gospel, the other deriving from natural law assumptions. From the perspective of the former war is the unambiguous sign of sin and can never be called a good. From the perspective of the latter war can sometimes be a good, indeed a moral duty, necessary to preserve human community. While not strictly incompatible it is not clear how one can hold both at once.

This is particularly true if one continues to maintain, as the Pastoral does, there can be no incompatibility between nature and grace, reason and revelation (17). For if just war is based on natural law, a law written in the conscience of all men and women by God, then it seems that war must be understood as the outgrowth of legitimate moral commitments. If war, however, is the compromise we make to sin then it is not clear on what grounds, given the Gospel ethic depicted by the Pastoral, Christians can participate in war. That is, it is not clear if one presumes that Christians should avoid intentionally cooperating with sin.

3. How Cooperation Results in War

Many, impressed with the universality of violence, attribute war to some fundamental aspect of human nature. The difficulty with such "explanations," however is they tell us little about the specific activity we call war. As Kenneth Waltz suggests, while human nature no doubt plays a part in bringing about war, it cannot "by itself explain both war and peace, except by the simple statement that man's nature is such that sometimes he fights and sometimes he does not."[11] In other words to say that war is the result of some aspect of human nature is at once to say too much and too little. Too much is said because it is unclear what possibly could count against such a claim. Too little, because concentration on the "primary" cause of war directs our attention away from an analysis of the relation between states. Attempts to explain war by appeals to human nature mistakenly assume that war has *a* cause.

As I suggested at the beginning, war is not simply violence in a magnified form. Rather, it is an institution which arises among peoples who can claim sufficient commonality to transform violence into power. As Hannah Arendt reminds us, power is an instrument of rule and thus is the mitigation of violence. [12] Power implies the ability of people to cooperate so that explicit violence is not needed. Violence is thus that to which individuals whether they be particular persons or foreign states, resort in order to challenge the legitimacy of power. [13] When power breaks down violence is often the result. Therefore, according to Arendt, power is indeed the essence of all government but violence is not. While we might call war violent, its essence is not violence for in a moral sense it is the enemy of violence.

War is an institution that occurs uniquely between agents of power. Currently we call such agents "nation-states" though war is by no means limited to that particular institution. War, for example, can occur between peoples who have not organized themselves into nations as we know them. War must be a continuing possibility between nation states (or other communities), since there neither is nor does it seem there ought to be a system of law, of power, enforceable between them.

Communities exist on the basis of shared public concern. Each state must judge its own interests and purposes in terms of its particular history and situation. As a result, to accept war is not to accept violence or anarchy; it is to accept commonality and cooperation.

In his now classic, *Man, the State, and War: a Theoretical Analysis,* Kenneth Waltz develops the moral assumptions behind this account of war by calling attention to Rousseau's analysis of the nature and the cause of war. According to Rousseau persons were originally dispersed sufficiently to make cooperation unnecessary. But numbers increased and contact with other humans posed the alternatives; cooperate or die. Rousseau illustrates this with the simplest example: "Assume that five men who have acquired a rudimentary ability to speak and to understand each other happen to come together at a time when all of them suffer from hunger. The hunger of each will be satisfied by the fifth part of a stag, so they 'agree' to cooperate in a project to trap one. But also the hunger of any one of them will be satisfied by a hare so, as a hare comes within reach, one of them grabs it. The defector obtains the means of satisfying his hunger but in doing so permits the stag to escape. His immediate interest prevails over consideration for his fellows."[14]

The example, while obviously overly simple, conveys a significant but often overlooked point. Unlike most who link conflict casually to some imperfection of our nature – particularly of our reason – Rousseau tries to show that the "sources of conflict are not so much in the minds of men as they are in the nature of social activity."[15] Conflict arises not from our individual selfishness, though we may be selfish, but from the nature of cooperation whereby one person's immediate interest and the general long-term interest of the group are not the same. Yet the long-term interest can be served only when all individuals concerned forgo their immediate interest. Yet it is not merely that each must forgo an immediate interest, but each must trust the others to do so as well. As Waltz points out, "The problem is now posed in more significant terms. If harmony is to exist in anarchy, not only must I be perfectly rational but I must be able to assume that everyone else is too."[16] But that is exactly what I cannot assume.

If the rational choice is to forgo the imme

diate good to cooperate, then rationality
entails the acceptance of the possibility of
coercion whereby the dissenting individual is
forced to serve the common good. This is the
moral importance of power; without it we
could not justify our pursuit of the common
good which in turn justifies all our attempts
at cooperation. From such a perspective
society (and resulting states) is a remarkable
moral achievement. For a state is a unit
created by establishing habits of trust through
which the citizen is encouraged to submit to
a general will for the good of the whole.
Whether the state is organic or only the name
of some power that has so established itself
so that its decisions are accepted as decisions
for all it is nonetheless a force for order. Compliance is rationally fortified by two consider-
ations: one does not have the power to change
the decision; and one judges that in the long
run it is to his or her advantage to cooperate
with the state's decision and work for change
in the accepted ways. According to Rousseau
the better the state the more prominent the
second consideration. [17]

The distillation of a cooperative venture
into a state allows for the further possibility
of cooperation/conflict between states. Here

unity is particularly important. For questions of foreign policy call for choices that are supported by the state as a whole. If a state is to have a foreign policy it must be able to speak at times with a single voice. War, therefore, is a particularly important time as in war states are most likely to be able to generate nearly unanimous backing. The unity of the nation, in fact, is partly derived from antagonism generated by international contact. Thus individuals participate in war because they are members of states and because only states can make war on other states. [18]

War is thus not to be immediately judged as good or evil any more then the man who pursues the hare. Contrary to the assumption of *Pacem in Terris* Rousseau has tried to show that even if all states were good states, that is, states which work to procure the uncoerced consent of their citizens, we would not necessarily have a world of peace. For the will of any one state is only a particular will in relation to another. The absence of any authority above states to prevent or adjust conflicts means that war is inevitable. Abstractly put this means "that among particularities accidents will occur is not accidental but necessary."[19]

Theoretically, we can imagine two alternatives to war: (1) impose an effective control on separate states or (2) remove states from the sphere of the accidental; that is, to define a state that is not particularly constituted. The former possibility is fraught with its own dangers; the extent of the power necessary for such control is frightening to us. The latter is impossible since states by their very nature are formed and "maintained by nothing better than chance."[20] Indeed our greatest danger comes when some states forget their particularity and claim universality and thus the right to determine the affairs of other states.[21]

The startling simple implication of Rousseau's analysis is that war occurs because there is nothing to prevent it. As we cannot presume all individuals will comply uncoerced with the common good of the state, so we cannot assume states will subordinate their ends. If we seek cooperation we must accept the possibility of war. Of course Rousseau's account does not purport to tell us how one or the other war is caused; surely in each case a wide range of circumstances and purposes is at work. Particular wars may be more or less justifiable, but war *per se* is never justifiably excluded as a possibility. War just is; it is neither good nor bad.

Perhaps from this perspective we can appreciate the ambiguity we often feel about war as an institution. We do not generally seek war; we think of it as something we choose when we have no other choice. Even though war is clearly human activity, we tend to conceive it as an external agent, a fate that we had not willed but which we cannot but follow. It is just in the "nature" of things. War is finally no one's fault; it is an unsolicited yet unavoidable consequence of our shared activities. War in this sense is simply beyond good and evil.

4. Should War Be Eliminated?

Rousseau has suggested that war is an unavoidable by-product of our cooperation. While in itself morally ambiguous, as a by-product of cooperation, its elimination would mean as well the extinction of cooperation. Therefore we should not seek to eliminate war.

But there are perhaps other reasons why war should not be eliminated, which are related to this, yet distinguishable from it.

These point to the moral purpose served specifically by war. We do not live in a world of a common morality. What goods we share are those that come to us through the achievement and sacrifices of our forebears. Our goods are inseparable from our histories and our histories can only be preserved as they are associated with states pledged to protect them. While no one wishes war, it may in some cases be the only way to preserve these goods.

Indeed in war we learn to sacrifice ourselves for these goods. No morality is worthy that does not require sacrificing even our life. War, also, teaches us to preserve the common life, even to kill for it, precisely because the common life transcends the life of the individual. Indeed to refuse to kill for the state would be to dishonor those who have given their lives for the morality that the state is pledged to protect. So when threatened the good state cannot but ask us to be willing to kill in the name of the good we have achieved.

Indeed the very achievements that we are often called upon to protect through the means of war are those that in the past have been achieved through war. We must pursue war exactly because not to do so dishonors those who have made us what we are through the sacrifices they have made in past wars. This is not simply to make the point that engagement in war breeds extraordinary camaraderie, although that is surely true. Rather it is to say, with Hegel, that it is only in time of war that the state achieves its true universality. For only then are "the rights and interests of individuals established as a passing phase."[22]

Yet I do not think Hegel has put it quite right, for it is not a matter simply of our individual interest's being qualified in times of war for the greater good. Rather war reaffirms our history by offering us the opportunity to be worthy of our history by making similar sacrifices. We fight wars because our ancestors have fought wars. Wars provide us a way to realize our continuity with our ancestors, to locate ourselves within their continuing saga, and in the process, to give to that saga an otherwise absent coherence over time.

There is no question that war makes marvelous history to read. We like to read about war, I think, not simply because there are sometimes good and bad guys, winners and losers, but because war, unlike most of

our lives, seems to be more coherent. To be
sure, in the middle of a battle the participants
seldom know what is going on or what they
are doing, but looking back on the confusion,
an order emerges that often reassures us
that, whether we won or lost, we still have
a damn fine story to tell. Not only to tell but
to be. It is a particular story to be sure, and
perhaps we tell it with a good deal of bias,
but it is nonetheless ours.

In that respect I sometimes think there is
a deep commonality between baseball and
war. I am hesitant to make such a suggestion
as it seems so frivolous if not immoral. War
is too serious for such comparisons. Yet just
as baseball seems to be played not for the
playing itself but for the gathering of statis-
tics so that we may later tell the story, so
wars seem to be fought so that we are able
to place ourselves within a framework that
gives us a place to be. We fear destruction,
but even more we fear not having a niche
within an ongoing history. War is our ultimate
comfort in a world without a history for it
provides us with a story. To be sure it may
be a hard and even gruesome story, but such
a story is better than no story at all.

I am not suggesting that we fight wars in

order to have a story to tell. Rather the stories that we learn to tell as peoples inextricably involve war as one of the major characters in the story. That this is the case perhaps helps us understand further why it is almost impossible to exclude war as an imaginative possibility from our lives. For if war is no longer a possibility we fear we will lose the ability to locate ourselves in a worthy story or as participants in the ongoing life of a people.

In summary, I have suggested that war is to provide for as well as sustain the particular goods of particular peoples in a divided world. War is not anarchy existing between states, but rather it is anarchy's enemy insofar as it allows corporate entities, such as the nation-states to perpetuate their own particular shared goods; to preserve their histories and moralities. Conflict in the international arena may not only arise as societies protect their histories but as they attempt to share them as well. Indeed it sometimes appears that nations with the most in common war the most frequently and bitterly, much as within families conflict is often the bitterest. As the ties of cooperation are strong so is the possibility of conflict; for, as I have argued, the two are inextricably related.

Such is the best case I can muster for the moral viability of war. It is obviously an ideal account as the sheer stupidity, mendacity, and perversity that often gets us into war is missing. That the presumption and idolatry of nation-states who assume their interests override all others, even those of the survival of the human species, is not taken into account. But the case I have tried to present is not meant to provide the discriminating judgments necessary to determine the wisdom of particular wars. Rather all I have done is to suggest why some find it so hard to exclude war as a moral possibility in human affairs. You can accept my analysis and still condemn particular wars as irrational, imprudent, or immoral. What you cannot do, if this account is right, is condemn a war on the grounds that all war is fundamentally immoral.

5. Peace, Justice, and the Viability of Pacifism

In the preceding sections I have done my best to give an account of war as a moral institution. But in what ways has it helped us understand why Christians so often say they are advocates of peace but accept the neces sity of war? Does it, for example, help us to understand why the bishops, in *The Challenge of Peace*, acknowledge the non-violent character of the Gospel while continuing to support Christian participation in war?

As we have seen the bishops suppose they must accept war as an inevitability in this time between the times. The peace brought by Jesus is an eschatological peace. It is God's gift and cannot be the work of humankind. While God's peace may provide the individual with a sense of future union with God, it cannot be the working principle for present relations between nations; it is at present but an ideal in a complex and fallen world. Some in the name of God's peace may personally renounce the use of all violence, but they can by no means stand as an example for nations or, for that matter, all Christians.

For the peace that is already ours in Christ is a religious not a political reality (55).[23] Committed as they are to this eschatological peace which is not just the absence of war but the peace that comes from justice, Christians cannot exclude the possibility of violence (68). So any pursuit of justice, any pursuit of a peace that is political, may require that Christians sadly use violence since "the struggle for

justice may threaten certain forms of peace"
(60).

For the bishops St. Augustine gave the
clearest answer to the question why Christians must resort to war even though they
desire peace. They, thus, tell us

> Augustine was impressed by the fact and the
> consequences of sin in history – the 'not yet'
> dimension of the kingdom. In his view war was
> both the result of sin and a tragic remedy for
> sin in the life of political societies. War arose
> from disordered ambitions, but it could also be
> used, in some cases at least to restrain evil and
> protect the innocent. The classic case which
> illustrated his view was the use of lethal force
> to prevent aggression against innocent victims.
> Faced with the fact of attack on the innocent,
> the presumption that we do no harm, even to
> our enemy, yielded to the command of love
> understood as the need to restrain an enemy
> who would injure the innocent. The just-war
> argument has taken several forms in the history
> of Catholic theology, but this Augustinian in-
> sight is its central premise" (81-82).

In a similar manner David Hollenbach has argued that for the just war theory the goods of peace and justice are interdependent. "Justice is regarded as the precondition of peace in the concrete political order. The pursuit of justice, even by force, can in some circumstances be the only way to fulfill the duty to promote both peace and justice."[24] Both Hollenbach and the bishops agree that the resort to war comes not from the counsel of Jesus, for to follow his non-violent example would be to collapse the tension between the already and not-yet of Christian eschatology. As long as we live in history there must exist an unresolved tension between justice and nonviolence. This tension requires the Christian to use violence in the cause of justice.[25]

The assumption that war can be a means for achieving justice, I think, entails a view of war very similar to the one I have developed. The bishops and Hollenbach assume a state has the responsibility to defend its people in the cause of justice. Yet what it means to "defend its people" is never made clear as wars are seldom fought to protect the physical survival of a people but rather for the achievement of this or that political advantage. Behind this question are complex questions

about the justification of just-war thinking.
For we are sometimes told that just-war
theory is derived from the analogy of self-
defense and at other times the primary
paradigm that justifies the use of violence is
the defense of the innocent. While these may
not be incompatible they can make a great
difference for how one understands the
nature and role of state power to prosecute
war. [26]

However if, as I have suggested, war is the
means a people have to protect not just their
existence but their interpretation of their
existence, then war in a sense does not need
a "justification." Perhaps that is why some
prefer to talk not about just war, but of justified war. [27] The justice war protects is the
cooperative achievement by a people that
often has been the result of their forebears'
waging war for limited moral goods. [28]

Aside from the individualistic analogy often
employed, we are reminded in this context
that just war theory is much more a theory
of state action than a justification of individual response to attack. In other words the
primary actor required by just-war thinking
is not the individual, but the state acting on
behalf of its society. Here the theory can be

correlated with my previous account. In a sense only the state has the right of self-defense for it alone has the responsibility of defending that history that makes a people a people. "The state" is the name we give to those charged with upholding the patterns of cooperation achieved by our society to preserve our particular shared goods. To preserve that cooperation and relative peace the state must be prepared to wage war against any who would threaten it. That is the "justice" that war protects.

This kind of interpretation of the "justice" of the state I think may be the necessary presumption to make clear why, in spite of a tacit affirmation of peace, the bishops continue to insist that nations have the right and duty to defend themselves against an unjust aggressor. But if this account is right, then I think the bishops need to be more candid than they have been about the status of peace. For I do not see how you can give nations the right to defend themselves and yet, at the same time, maintain that peace is not only the ideal but the normal state of affairs between nations. For are you not required to recognize that such a "peace" is but that justice dependent on the continued possibility of war?[29]

In this respect I do not see how the bishops can maintain, as they try to do, the right of some to be non-violent. That they do so is of course extraordinary; imagine Roman Catholics ever hinting that pacifism is an option as appropriate for Christians as just war. Yet surely an affirmation of pacifism cannot but seriously qualify the bishops' defense of just war as not merely the means of peace but also as the form just peace must take in this time between the times.

The bishops, however, are very careful in their support for the pacifist position. For they are very clear that their support is for the pacifist options for "individuals" (119). Moreover they suggest that this "new moment" determined by our possession of nuclear weapons has meant an increasing convergence between pacifist and just-war positions. For "they share a common presumption against the use of force as a means of settling disputes. Both find their roots in the Christian theological tradition; each contributes to the full moral vision we need in pursuit of a human peace. We believe the two perspectives support and complement one another, each preserving the other from distortion" (120-121). At any rate, the bishops never propose, nor can they propose, pacifism as an option for statecraft. [30]

Rev. Hollenbach is even more adamant in his support of pacifism as an option for some Christians. Both pacifism and just-war positions are necessary if

> the full content of Christian hope is to be made visible in history. Each of these ethical stances bears witness to an essential part of the Christian mystery. Each of them, however, is incomplete by itself. Within time it is simply not possible to embody the fullness of the kingdom of God in a single form of life or a single ethical standard. Thus if the Christian community is to be faithful to the full meaning of the paschal mystery as the inauguration of the kingdom of God, there must be a pluralism of ethical stances represented within it. I would conclude, therefore, that both the pacifist and the just war ethic are legitimate and necessary expressions of the Christian faith. The necessity of such pluralism in approaching the morality of warfare is a particular case of the more general theological truth that the kingdom of God cannot be fully expressed in any single historical way of living or hierarchy of values. Pacifism and just war theory are both historical syntheses of a particular aspect of the Christian hope with an historical-political interpretation of how the basic values of justice and peace are related to each other within time. The fact that these two

traditions have been present within the Christian community for millennia has not been an accident but a theological necessity.[31]

Thus those that adhere to just war need the pacifist to remind them of the centrality of nonviolence that is too easily lost amid the intricacies of public policy debates. The pacifist on the other hand needs the just war representatives to remind them of the centrality of justice and that Christian responsibility can never be limited simply by avoiding evil but requires the positive promotion of both justice and peace.

It may seem terribly ungrateful for me as a pacifist to argue against this unusual acceptance of the pacifist position, but I think there are important reasons for doing so; or more accurately I fear that the approval of pacifism as a stance for individuals may seem to put the bishops more firmly on the side of peace than they are. They seem to support pacifism when in fact the structure of their argument ought to lead them to be more candid about their support of war. If, as they maintain, it is not just a right, but a duty of a state to defend itself through the force of arms, pacifists act irresponsibly insofar as they absent themselves from the joint moral undertaking which the state must perform.

Of course in times of peace it may be that the state has the resources sufficient to give some the privilege to follow their conscience against war. Such a policy can make sense on a number of pragmatic grounds since such people may make poor soldiers or to grant them exemption from military service may result in taking some of the moral heat off the military. Yet it is difficult to understand how a state can perpetuate such a policy when its existence is being threatened if in fact, as the Pastoral argues, a people threatened with unjust aggression "may not remain passively indifferent" (76).

In spite of the general statements about peace in the Pastoral it continues to assume that those that would take the pacifist stance, even as individuals, bear the burden of proof. They bear the burden of proof because, the bishops presume, states are the bearers of our history, and nations (as I have argued) rely upon war or the possibility of war to sustain our history. Indeed the assumption that the state bears our history leads straight to the affirmation that war is not just a necessity caused by sin, but an institution morally necessary for the protection of the goods of a society. And if it is such then those that refuse to go to war have made a decisive moral mistake.

Although Hollenbach tends to interpret the difference between just-war and pacifist positions primarily in strategic terms, he as well must give a secondary status to pacifism. The pacifist tradition "argues the non-theological part of its case against the just war on a competing historical-political interpretation of the relation between non-violence and justice. It maintains the use of force inevitably contributes to an escalating spiral of both violence and injustice."[32] While the advent of nuclear weapons has certainly given new weight to this pacifist position, nonetheless it cannot be the last word on violence for the Christian since it cannot "be made the basis for a political ethic for a pluralist society."[33] In contrast the just war is an attempt to consider how the "basic values of life, freedom, justice, etc. are related to each other in the light of our historical experience and our practical understanding of the political order."[34] Thus the ultimate problem with pacifists is that they are "prepared to tolerate injustice in the limit situation where justice cannot be attained by non-violent means."[35]

Hollenbach's account, therefore, seems but another version of the suggestion that the pacifist is useful to remind those that are really concerned about justice that violence may finally be self-defeating, but pacifism cannot be a stance of the church. The crucial claim by Hollenbach is that pacifism cannot be made the political ethic for a pluralist society, that is, a society that has its being shaped and protected by war. For the "just war theory, the goods of peace and justice are interdependent, but justice is regarded as the precondition of peace in the concrete political order. The pursuit of justice, even by force, can in some circumstances be the only way to fulfill the duty to promote both peace and justice."[36]

The affirmation of pluralism, however, is not as free from costs as Hollenbach suggests. For it appears that by embracing both pacifism and just war theory he can provide the means to achieve justice in a pluralist society. He assumes such a society is so significant the gospels' command of peace can be qualified in the interest of the "justice" such a society represents.

I do not think, therefore, that Hollenbach can resolve the tension between pacifist and just-war theorist as easily as he suggests. He, and the bishops, want on the one hand to say the just war is the attempt to set down the "conditions under which exceptions to the

general obligation to non-violence might be
made," and there is certainly some truth to
that.[37] But on the other hand, they want to
maintain that war is the character of our lives
"between the times" as the failure to go to war
cannot but result in injustice. From this latter
perspective the just war theory is not just a
theory of exceptions, but an attempt to limit
the destructive potential of war once it is
recognized as a moral necessity. As such just
war, as a theory, denies pacifism; it does not
attempt to make war impossible, but rather to
make the moral necessity of war serve human
purposes. As such it would seem that the bishops and Hollenbach should welcome the account I have tried to give concerning why war
cannot morally be eliminated from our lives.

6. The Elimination of War:
A Theological Imperative

By developing a moral case for war I have
tried to help us understand ambivalence about
war among Christians. We say we want peace
yet we still hold out the possibility of war. I
have taken *The Challenge of Peace* as a prime
example of this ambivalence as the bishops,
who strive to take the Gospel imperatives for

peace so seriously, seem yet unable to free
themselves from the assumption that Christians must still be willing to support war in
the interest of justice. Such ambivalence takes
form in eschatological appeals to our living
between the times when our ideals must be
compromised by the recognition of our sinful
condition. Thus the bishops uphold the right,
if not duty, of nations to defend themselves
thereby underwriting the hold war has over
our imaginations. While we all want to mini-
mize war in general, we will not relinquish the
possibility of war for our national communities. We do so not simply because we believe
we live in a sinful world, but because we
believe that our nations are the bearers of
commitments and goods which justice com-
pels us to defend even if such defense requires
war. We wish for peace but plan for war; and
we get it.

My analysis, I believe, pushes the bishops
in the direction of supporting war, a direction
that they clearly want to avoid. To this it may
be objected that I have treated the bishops
unfairly as they give every indication that
they wish to rid the world of war.[38] Quoting
John Paul II, they say, "Today, the scale and
the horror of modern warfare — whether

nuclear or not – makes it totally unacceptable as a means of settling differences between nations. War should belong to the tragic past, to history; it should find no place on humanity's agenda for the future" (21). Surely by criticizing nuclear weapons the bishops do not mean to encourage war. Moreover they underwrite the concern to develop non-violent ways for conflict resolution rejecting the argument that pacifists have no response to violence (221-230). Yet one must question how seriously such suggestions are to be taken as long as the bishops unwaveringly affirm that Christians can in times of stress resort to violence. As long as the bishops entertain the moral possibility of war I cannot see how they can avoid its actuality.

But did they (and do we) have an alternative? I believe we do. It is an alternative to which the bishops point in their sensitive portrayal of the peace brought by Jesus' life, death, and resurrection. Such a peace, as the bishops quite rightly note, is not simply the absence of war, but it is rather a peace that is itself an alternative to a world at war. As such it is not as some ideal, but is an actual way of life among a concrete group of people. The bishops are quite right, it is an eschatological peace, but they are wrong to think it can be ours only on the "edge of history." Rather it means that we must see peace as a possibility amid a world at war.[39] The decisive issue is how we understand the eschatological nature of God's peace. The bishops stress the "already but not yet" as a way of legitimating Christian participation in war. But, as the bishops also indicate, to view the world eschatologically does not mean simply to mark the kingdom as yet to come for in fact the kingdom has been made present fully in Jesus Christ. That is why they rightly say Jesus' words requiring us to forgive one another, the requirement to love our enemy more than all others, are not just ideals but possibilities here and now (45-48). Thus Jesus "made the tender mercy of God present in a world that knew violence, oppression and injustice" (15).

God's "tender mercy" is not a sense of forgiveness that comes after we have had to use violence for justice, though such forgiveness certainly is not withheld, but rather his "tender mercy" makes it possible to stand against the world's tragic assumption that war can be the means to justice. To be sure, here a different understanding of eschatology

is at work than that of the bishops, but I
believe it is one that is closer to that of the
New Testament. For the bishops seem to
have accepted the view that the early Christians were non-violent only because they had
a mistaken apocalyptic idea that the world
was soon to end. When that end failed to ar-
rive Christians reluctantly took up the means
of violence in the interest of justice. In fact
what we now know of the New Testament
eschatology differs from such a view. To be
sure, the early Christians looked for God's
reign immediately to become a reality for all
people, but that did not qualify their dedica-
tion to live in that reign here and now.[40]

The eschatology of the New Testament
rests not in the conviction that the kingdom
has not fully come, but that it has. What is
required is not a belief in some ideal amid the
ambiguities of history, but rather a recognition that we have entered a period in which
two ages overlap. As John Howard Yoder has
observed "These aeons are not distinct
periods of time, for they exist simultaneously.
They differ rather in nature or in direction;
one points backwards to human history out-
side of (before) Christ; the other points for-
ward to the fullness of the kingdom of God,

of which it is a foretaste. Each aeon has a social manifestation: the former in the 'world,' the latter in the body of Christ."[41]

The Christian commitment to non-violence is therefore not first of all an "ethic" but a declaration of the reality of the new age. Again as Yoder puts it,

> Non-resistance is thus not a matter of legalism but of discipleship, not 'thou shalt not' but 'as he is so are we in this world' (I Jn. 4:17), and it is especially in relation to evil that discipleship is meaningful. Every strand of New Testament literature testifies to a direct relationship between the way Christ suffered on the cross and the way the Christian, as disciple, is called to suffer in the face of evil (Mt. 10:38; Mk. 10:38f; 8:34f: Lk. 14:27). Solidarity with Christ ("discipleship") must often be in tension with the wider human solidarity. (Jn. 15:20; II Cor. 1:5; 4:10; Phil. :29). It is not going too far to affirm that the new thing revealed in Christ was this attitude to the old aeon including force and self-defense. The cross was not in itself a new revelation; Isaiah 53 foresaw already the path which the Servant of Jahweh would have to tread. Nor was the resurrection essentially new; God's victory over evil had been affirmed, by definition one might say, from the beginning. Nor was the selection of a faithful remnant a new idea. What was centrally new about Christ was that these ideas became incarnate. But superficially the

greatest novelty and the occasion of stumbling
was His willingless to sacrifice, in the interest
of non-resistant love, all other forms of human
solidarity, including the legitimate national
interests of the chosen people. The Jews had
been told that in Abraham all the nations would
be blessed and had understood this promise as
the vindication of their nationalism. Jesus
revealed that the contrary was the case: the
universality of God's kingdom contradicts rather
than confirms all particular solidarities and can
be reached only by first forsaking the old aeon.
(Lk. 18: 28-30).[42]

So in spite of the bishops' (and Hollenbach's)
attempt to clear a space for the pacifist I cannot accept the terms of their acceptance. For
pacifism and just war are not simply two ethical
strategies for the achievement of God's justice
in the world. Rather they draw on different
assumptions about history and its relation to
God's kingdom. The debate between pacifism
and just-war thinking is a theological issue of
how we are to read and interpret history. I have
argued that war is part and parcel of societies'
histories, a necessary part which provides them
with their sense of moral purpose and destiny.
The problem with those histories is not they are
devoid of moral substance, but they are not
God's history. They are not the way God would

have his kingdom present in the world. The debate between pacifism and just-war thinking is, therefore, a theological question of how we are to read and interpret history.

Christians believe that the true history of the world, that history that determines our destiny, is not carried by the nation-state. In spite of its powerful moral appeal, this history is the history of godlessness. Only the church has the stance, therefore, to describe war for what it is, for the world is too broken to know the reality of war. [43] For what is war but the desire to be rid of God, to claim for ourselves the power to determine our meaning and destiny? Our desire to protect ourselves from our enemies, to eliminate our enemies in the name of protecting the common history we share with our friends, is but the manifestation of our hatred of God. [44]

Christians have been offered the possibility of a different history through participation in a community in which one learns to love the enemy. They are thus a people who believe that God will have them exist through history without the necessity of war. God has done so by providing the world with a history through the church. For without the church we are but a scattered people with nothing in common. Only through the church do we learn that we share that same creator and destiny. So the world's true history is not that built on war, but that offered by a community that witnesses to God's refusal to give up on his creation.

This does not mean that our existence is constituted by two histories. There is only one true history – the history of God's peaceable kingdom. Christians can admit no ultimate dualism between God's history and the world's history. The peace we believe we have been offered is not just for us but it is the peace for all, just as we believe our God is the God of all. Thus we do not preclude the possibility that a state could exist for which war is not a possibility. To deny such a possibility would be the ultimate act of unbelief for who are we to determine the power of God's providential care of the world. [45]

Christians, therefore, offer a "moral equivalent to war" in William James' sense by first offering themselves. James rightly saw that the essential problem for the elimination of war lies in our imagination. Under the power of the history created by war we cannot morally imagine a world without war. But James' suggestion that we find new contexts to sustain the virtues which arise in war is too weak. What is required is not simply discovering new contexts to sustain martial virtues, but rather an alternative history. Precisely this God has offered through the life, death, and resurrection of Jesus of Nazareth. Such an alternative is not an unrealizable ideal. No, it is present now in the church, a real alternative able to free our imagination from the capacity of war.

For the imagination is not simply a container of images or ideas that we now entertain in preference to other images and ideas. Rather the imagination is a set of habits and relations that can only be carried by a group of people in distinction from the world's habits. For example nothing is more important for the church's imagination than the meal we share together in the presence of our crucified and resurrected Lord. For it is in that meal, that set of habits and relations, that the world is offered an alternative to the habits of disunity on which war breeds.

In the practice of such a meal we can see that the morality that makes war seem so necessary to our lives is deeply flawed. For it is a morality that sees no alternative to war as the necessary means to sustain our parti-

cular loyalties. It leads us to suppose those
loyalties can be protected, we think, only by
eliminating the threat of the other, be it aggression or merely strangeness. But in the
meal provided by the Lord of history we dis-
cover our particularity is not destroyed but
enhanced by the coming of the stranger. In
the church we find an alternative to war exactly because there we learn to make others'
histories part of our own. We are able to do
so because God has shown us the way by
making us a new people through the life,
death, and resurrection of Jesus Christ.[46]

From this perspective "Should war be
eliminated?" is a false question. It is not a false
question because the elimination of war is
impossible or because war has a moral viability that means we should not eliminate it.
Rather it is a false question because war has
been eliminated for those that participate in
God's history. The miracle we call the church
is God's sign that war is not part of his providential care of the world. Our happy task as
Christians is to witness to that fact.

But perhaps all this misses the point. To say
the church is the carrier of a history otherwise
than the history of war sounds lofty, but in
fact we know we do not live in such a history.

We continue to live in a history determined by nation-states where war shows no signs of abating. Even worse it is a world now threatened by nuclear annihilation. Do Christians, because of their commitment to peace, say that is too bad for the world and let others do their fighting for them? Or do they follow the Augustinian solution noting that the two histories are hopelessly mixed together on this side of the eschaton so we are required to use the means of violence to support the history of the world?

Once again we have arrived at a false alternative. Christian commitment to non-violence does not require withdrawal from the world and the world's violence. Rather it requires the Christian to be in the world with an enthusiasm that cannot be defeated, for he or she knows that the power of war is not easily broken. Christians, therefore, cannot avoid, just as the bishops have not tried to avoid, attempting one step at a time to make the world less war determined. We do that exactly by entering into the complex world of deterrence and disarmament strategy believing that a community nutured on the habits of peace might be able to see new opportunities not otherwise present. For what creates new opportunities is being a kind of people who have been freed from the assumption that war is our fate.

Christian commitement to non-violence is a way of life for the long haul. Exactly because we understand how morally compelling war can be we know what a challenge we face. That is why we offer the world not simply moral advice designed to make war less destructive, but rather a witness to God's invitation to join a community that is so imaginative, so rich in its history, that it gives us the means to resist the temptation to give our loyalties to those that would use them for war. At Babel we were scattered each having our own language and history, and even those who followed Jesus were scattered prior to his death, yet in his resurrection we have been gathered again to be part of God's history. In him we have our peace, by his grace we can be of good cheer since he has overcome the world (John 16: 32-33). [47]

NOTES

1. George Kennan, *The Nuclear Delusion: Soviet-American Relations in the Atomic Age* (New York: Pantheon Books, 1983), p. 243.

2. The classic account of this perspective on war is J. Glenn Grey's, *The Warriors: Reflections on Men in Battle* (New York: Harper Torchbook, 1970). For a recent attempt to defend the vocation of the soldier see Walter Benjamin, "In Defense of the Soldier," *Christianity and Crisis* 43, 19 (November 28, 1983), pp. 453-458; and my response in the same issue, "What Can the State Ask?"

3. *The Challenge of Peace: God's Promise and Our Response* (Washington, D.C., United States Catholic Conference, 1983). All references to the Pastoral will appear in the text and refer to the numbered paragraph.

4. It is often alleged, moreover, if one is a pacifist then one really has nothing to say of interest about war. For example the Harvard Nuclear Study Group begins its "The Realities of Arms Control" with the claim, "In an imperfect world, few people have been willing to adopt pure pacifism, which means the refusal to defend one's self, family, country, or allies from any kind of attack. Those who are not pacifists must wrestle with many difficult choices about weapons, their existence, and their potential use. This has always been true. Warfare is as old as human history, and disarmament as a prescription for avoiding it dates back at least to biblical times." *Atlantic Monthly* 251, 6 (June, 1983), p. 39. The implication that pacifists simply have nothing to say about war or strategies of disarmament is a silent rebuke suggesting that pacifists simply do not face up to the hard issues. But the pacifist, no less than the just-war advocate, must be concerned to find means to make war less likely and less destructive.

After all the pacifist refusal to participate in war does not mean that all wars are therefore morally on a par. Indeed it is even more a moral imperative for the pacifist to be concerned with issues of how disarmament can take place since the pacifist knows that calls for peace apart from an account of how such peace might take place cannot but appear as utopian.

5. John XXIII, *Peace on Earth* (Huntington, Indiana: Our Sunday Visitor, 1965). All references will be in the text and to the numbered paragraph. I am treating *Peace on Earth* not only because it provides the necessary background for understanding the Pastoral of the American Bishops. For the bishops' appeal to just war seems to presuppose the kind of reasoning suggested by *Peace on Earth*. Indeed Bryan Hehir suggests that the Pastoral is an attempt to blend *Peace on Earth* with the methodology of the Second Vatican Council's "Pastoral Constitution on the Church in the Modern World." See his "From the Pastoral Constitution of Vatican II to the Challenge of Peace" in *Catholics and Nuclear War,* edited by Philip Murnion (New York: Crossroad, 1983), 71-86.

6. For an extremely helpful account of Enlightment accounts of war and peace see W B. Gallie, *Philosophers of Peace and War: Kant, Clausewitz, Marx, Engels and Tolstoy* (Cambridge: Cambridge University Press, 1978).

Of course one of the crucial issues that too often goes unanalyzed in most of the literature dealing with war is whether we know what we mean when we say "state." Obviously a "state" is not the same as a people nor is it clear that a nation-state corresponds to what was classically meant by a "state" – that is a sub-unit for the government of a society. One wonders if the Enlightenment accounts of "state", which seem to be accepted in *Pacem in Terris* have any relation to what empirically counts for state in the modern world.

SHOULD WAR BE ELIMINATED?

7. The bishops' account of war in the Hebrew scriptures unfortunately is not well developed. It as if they admitted that war is seen as a valid mode of God's way with Israel, but fortunately we have the New Testament to balance that emphasis. If they had attended to such work as Millard Lind's *Yahweh Is a Warrior: The Theology of Warfare in Ancient Israel* (Scottsdale, Pennsylvania: Herald Pres, 1980) they would have been able to see a much stronger continuity between Israel and Jesus on the question of war.

8. There is an ambiguity in the bishops' position for it is not clear if the peace Jesus brought is not relevant for nuclear war because it is an eschatological peace or because Jesus did not speak explicitly about questions of nuclear war. I doubt the bishops would want to press the latter argument since there are many matters on which they want to speak authoritatively, e.g., contraception, on which Jesus did not speak explicitly.

9. Paragraphs 16 and 17 of the Pastoral give the most extended justification for the assumption that the pastoral should address the public policy debate on its own terms. Even within the presumption of the bishops, however, the matter is still fraught with ambiguity. For it is not clear if they want to enter the public debate because Catholics are "also members of the wider political community" and may thus be in positions of public responsibility about such matters; or if they want to address all people of good will. If the latter then it seems they are right to think they must presuppose a natural law starting point – that is, "a law written on the human heart by God" – that provides moral norms all can agree on irrespective of their faith. If the former, it is not clear why they cannot continue to speak theologically without resorting to natural law. The reason such issues are important is it is not clear the bishops can have it both ways. For at least they want in principle to claim that while the

norms of natural law do not "exhaust the gospel vision," neither are such norms in fundamental conflict with the obligation of Christians to follow Christ. Yet they also suggest that just war may be the kind of thinking necessary in a sinful world and thus less than the full demand of, and perhaps even a compromise with, the Gospel. This formal issue is reflected by the political ambiguity of the Pastoral. For example, David J. O'Brien observes,

> The bishops are caught in a classic bind. If they ground themselves exclusively in the scriptural imperative of love and withdraw from the effort to influence the public consensus and public policy, they may indeed mobilize considerable support for a critical, prophetic witness within the church, even if it costs the church many members and opens the community to charges of public irresponsibility. At the other extreme, they may stand too closely to the prevailing framework of responsibility, looking at issues through the lens of decision makers, become sympathetic to their dilemmas, and accept only the limited alternatives that seem to be presently available. If they move one way they seem utopian, unrealistic, and irresponsible. If they move the other they appear to have lost their integrity as Christian leaders acquiescing in situations they themselves have defined as unjust and immoral. "American Catholics and American Society," in *Catholics and Nuclear War,* p. 27.

10. In defense of the Bishops on this point Dennis McCann says,

> Lest the bishops be dismissed as at best muddled and at worst hypocritical we must recognize that within the Catholic tradition moral questions have never been exhausted by referring to the real or imagined ethic of Jesus. Later developments within the Christian ethos, beyond the time of

Jesus and the early Christians, are regarded as themselves part of the promise 'gift of the Spirit.' Without preempting the discussion of the bishops' 'quasi-theological beliefs,' here I must point out that when Catholic tradition adopted the paradigm of just war theory and began to transform it according to its own agenda, the transition was not marked by tortuous equivocation but by a new sense of what 'the call of Jesus' requires 'in context of the world as it presently exists.' The use of lethal force, in other words, came to be regarded as the most effective and the least unacceptable way 'to prevent aggression against innocent victims.' The paradigm of just war theory became morally necessary, as soon as Catholic tradition, following St. Augustine, admitted that war itself was not just the result of sin but also a 'tragic remedy for sin in the life of political societies.' "
"The NCCB Letter and Its Critics: An Ethical Analysis," in *Christian Perspectives in Nuclear Deterrence* edited by Bernard Adeney (Forthcoming).

Later McCann says such a position is justified by the trinitarian vision of the Pastoral as such a vision is obviously "larger than the words and deeds of Jesus of Nazareth. While such is and will ever remain the decisive moment of incarnation in history, that moment has meaning only in the context of the whole process. The mystery of God's Trinitarian presence thus is reflected in the overall pattern of meaning discerned in human life: we are to 'take responsibility for his work of creation and try to shape it in the ways of the kingdom." McCann, thus, seems to suggest that "just war" is a further development of the spirit, but surely that is an extremely doubtful claim. It may be that the trinitarian vision is larger than the words and deeds of Jesus, but I do not see how it can be claimed that vision is not in essential continuity with all Jesus said and did. In truth the bishops seem torn between justifying just war as a necessary compromise for living responsibly in a sinful world or as, as *Peace on Earth* suggests, a position consistent with natural law.

11. Kenneth Waltz, *Man, The State, and War: A Theoretical Analysis* (New York: Columbia University Press, 1959), p. 29.

12. Hannah Arendt, *On Violence* (New York: Harcourt, Brace, and World, Inc., 1970), p.36.

13. Ibid., p. 47.

14. Waltz, pp. 167-168.

15. Ibid., p. 168.

16. Ibid., p. 169.

17. Ibid., p. 178.

18. Ibid., p. 179.

19. Ibid., p. 182

20. Ibid., p. 183.

21. I think it is not accidental that the two most imperialistic states in the world today, U.S.A. and the USSR, are both founded on the universalistic assumptions of the Enlightenment.

22. Quoted by Michael Walzer in his *Obligations: Essays on Disobedience, War, and Citizenship* (New York: Simon and Schuster, 1970), p. 184.

23. In the light of the influence of liberation theology this claim seems a bit surprising; or at least one would have expected the bishops to provide a more elaborate defense. For if they wish to claim that the Gospel is political concerning matters of justice then I do not see how they can limit the Gospel's admonitions for peace to the "religious" realm.

24. David Hollenbach, *Nuclear Ethics: A Christian Moral Argument* (New York: Paulist Press, 1983), pp. 22-23. I introduce Rev. Hollenbach's work at this point, as he has spelled out more fully the position the bishops

have taken in the Pastoral. I do not want, however, to claim that his views are identical with that of the Pastoral.

25. Though the bishops and Hollenbach urge non-violent forms of resistance in the interest of justice they always hold out the possibility of violence if non-violence does not work. Yet they fail to give any indication how we are ever to know if non-violence has not worked and thus we can turn to violence. I suspect behind their failure to press this issue is the assumption that war is of the essence of state action so the ability of a state to use non-violence is extremely limited. They owe us an account, however, of how a Christian can do justice to the neighbor if we use the means that tell the neighbor that they are less obligated than we to love the enemy. For the "innocent" that we defend cannot be defended "justly" if the form of the defense belies our conviction, based on Jesus' way of dealing with the world, that the enemy is to be loved even as they attack. Peace and justice are not equal "means" for the building of God's kingdom, but rather the justice that required the forgiveness of enemies that makes peace possible is the kingdom.

26. For a fuller analysis of the significance of which of these pagadigms are primary for developing a justification of just-war thinking see my, "On Surviving Justly: An Ethical Analysis of Nuclear Disarmament," in Religious Conscience and Nuclear Warfare, edited by Jill Raitt (Columbia: University of Missouri, 1982), pp. 1-20. Paul Ramsey has argued the strongest for the paradigm of defense of the innocent for justification of just-war logic. I suspect that is why Ramsey places so much emphasis on the principle of discrimination as the overriding criterion for the justifiability of war. The bishops, unfortunately, seem to move uncritically from appeals to self-defense to defense of the innocent without noting how they make a difference for how one derives the various criteria of just

war or their priority. The analysis of war I have provided, however, is meant to provide them a way out
of this difficulty. For in effect they can say the justification of just war for a nation state can be put in the
language of self-defense because its larger intention
is to defend the innocent within the state. Therefore
the fundamental intention of just war at an individual
level is defense of the innocent, but as a social policy
it appears in the form of "self"-defense but the "self"
is a public agent.

27. See, for example, Paul Ramsey, *The Just War* (New
York: Scribner's Sons, 1968), pp. 4-18

28. That is why the criteria of discrimination may not be
overriding for a state's prosecution of war since the
task is to protect the past goods achieved by war.
Therefore, from a just war perspective the bishops
may be right to suggest that the principle of propor-
tionality is just as, if not more, important than discrimination for determining the morality of nuclear
warfare.

29. In his *The Just War: Force and Political Responsibility*
Paul Ramsey is admirably clear that the great task
is to save war and politics for purposeful use by
mankind. Therefore, the task is not to make war
impossible, but to make it serve human ends through
disciplining it through a politics formed by just-war
commitments. Therefore just war is commensurate
with the assumption that war is not the exception in
international relations but the norm. The bishops,
however, drawing on the assumptions of *Pacem in
Terris* seem to presume that war is the exception. I
am simply suggesting that their position would be
more consistent if they had followed Ramsey's lead.

30. Michael Novak, unlike the bishops, denies that
pacifism, even of an individual sort, is required by the
New Testament. The peace offered by Jesus is not the
absence of war, but a form of knowing and being in
union with God. It is a mistake, though one that is

honored, to believe we are called to imitate Jesus' non-violence, as it is a misreading of scripture as well as the Catholic tradition. Novak argues we must "sharply distinguish between pacifism as a personal commitment, implicating only a person who is not a public figure responsible for the lives of others, and pacifism as a public policy, compromising many who are not pacifists and endangering the very possibility of pacifism itself. It is not justice if the human race as a whole or in part is heaped with indignities, spat upon, publicly humiliated, destroyed, as Jesus was. It is not moral to permit the human race so to endure the injustice of the passion and death of Christ." *Moral Clarity in the Nuclear Age* (Nashville: Thomas Nelson, 1983), p. 34. Novak's argument is to the point, but I think he has not pressed it consistently enough. For why does he not argue further that Jesus was wrong to allow himself to die at the hands of such injustice? Or why not argue that at least the disciples should have come to Jesus' aid since Jesus' teaching should have convinced them that their overriding duty was to aid the innocent against injustice. One cannot but feel that those that defend so strongly the use of violence in the service of justice are finally trying to rescue Jesus from the cross. See, for example, Carl Oglesby, "Rescuing Jesus from the Cross," *The CoEvolution Quarterly*, 39 (Fall, 1983), pp. 36-41

It is not easy to characterize the difference between Novak's position and that of the bishops for it is not simply a difference about how to understand the facts and strategic alternatives. Rather it involves profound assumptions about the status of the just war theory as well as where one begins reflection on the ethics of war. Novak, unlike the bishops, does not assume you can begin with the just-war criteria and then ask in a legalistic way whether nuclear strategy conforms or does not conform to those criteria. Rather one must begin with an interpretation on the international

situation which relativizes the status of the just war
theory. Thus he says, "virtually all arguments about
the prevention of nuclear war hinge on judgments concerning the nature of the Soviet Union and its nuclear
forces" (p. 49). Even apart from the question of
whether Novak's account of the Soviet Union and his
depiction of the international situation is correct he
has not given us moral reasons for why we should
begin our ethical analysis of nuclear war with the
international context. Indeed, given Novak's account
it is extremely unclear why he bothers to treat the just
war theory at all. For a more detailed critique of
Novak's views, particulary his rather odd view of
"intention" see James Cameron, "Nuclear Catholics,"
New York Review of Books, xxx, 20. (December 22,
1983), pp. 38-42.

31. Hollenbach, p. 31.

32. Ibid., p. 43. Hollenbach, therefore, at least seems to
suggest that pacifism might be a social policy.

33. Ibid., p. 43. Like the bishops, Hollenbach assumes that
the church's social ethics must be one amenable to the
non-Christian. Yet, he confuses that issue with the
claims that Christian convictions must be capable of
being construed in policy terms. The latter may be
possible without those strategies being agreeable to
non-Christians.

34. Ibid., p. 43. The problem with such claims is that such
values are so abstractly put that we cannot be sure
what institutional form they may assume. It may be
that some who argue against nuclear war because it
threatens survival itself are right to remind us that
values such as freedom can be idolatrous when they
make our very survival problematic.

35. Ibid., p. 28.

36. Ibid., p. 23. Hollenbach's basic mistake is to think that
justice and peace are the means to build the kingdom
rather than the form of the kingdom itself.

37. Ibid., p. 37

38. I may have been particularly unfair to the bishops by treating what is essentially a political document as if it should be conceptually coherent. Indeed, in many ways the document is stronger exactly because it is a hodge-podge of different positions representing the different viewpoints of the various bishops. Yet the bishops say they want to be true to the intent of the Gospel and as much as I am able, I want to help them do just that.

39. For a marvelous account of a spirituality of peace see Rowan Williams, The *Truce of God* (New York: The Pilgrim Press, 1984). One of Rev. Williams' strongest themes is that peace is not simply what is left when social constraints have all vanished. Such a conception of peace he rightly criticizes as infantile, for the world created by such a peace is one where nothing happens and nothing is left to do. Rather the peace that is identified with Christian reconciliation is that which requires change and newness of life, not only of the heart, but in the structures of politics and industry, p. 58.

40. For a fuller defense of this view see my, *The Peaceable Kingdom: A Primer in Christian Ethics* (Notre Dame, IN: University of Notre Dame Press, 1983).

In his "The Moral Methodology of the Bishops' Pastoral," Charles Curran suggests that "much New Testament moral teaching is influenced by the eschatological coloring of the times; that is, many thought that the end of history was coming quickly, and such an understanding obviously colored their approach to moral questions. However, our understanding of eschatology is quite different. It is our understanding that the end-time has begun in Christ Jesus but will be completed only in his second-coming." *Catholics and Nuclear War,* p. 47. While I doubt the simplicity of Curran's description of early Christian attitudes about eschatology, I still do not see why he thinks that makes a difference about how Christians are to understand the New Testament. For the early Christians did not think they refrained from violence because the end of history was soon to come, but rather they refrained from violence because, as Curran suggests, they thought the end time had come.

One cannot but feel an uneasiness on the part of many Catholic moralists about the methodology of the Pastoral. The "conservatives" cannot but be worried about the implications for other questions of the moral life. For if you are willing to appeal to the ambiguity of the moral case caused by sin then why not apply the same moral logic to abortion. The "liberals" may rejoice in that result, but yet they may at the same time wish the bishops had been more forthright in their condemnation of nuclear war.

41. John Howard Yoder, *The Original Revolution* (Scottsdale, Pennsylvania: Herald Press, 1971), p. 58

42. Yoder, pp. 60-61.

43. The account of war I developed above is parasitic on Christian presupposition insofar as a unity of human history is presupposed from which war could be described. But, in fact, there is no such unity in history other than that provided by the church. Otherwise war is relative to each people's history. We thus often seek to deny to the other side the right to describe their violence as war. For example barbarians cannot be warriors since they do not fight in a civilized manner; a bombing in London by the IRA is terrorism not war. From this perspective war can be seen as a progressive conversation between diverse peoples about the meaning of war itself. World war is a moral achievement as it suggests all sides have the right to describe their violence as war. In so far as nuclear weapons force all to have a stake in war they can be seen as a moral advance reflecting our increasing interdependence.

44. For an unrelenting account of war along these lines see Dale Aukerman, *Darkening Vally* (New York: Seabury Press, 1981). Aukerman observes,

> The dual drives to be rid of God and the countering brother – the opposite of the dual loves to which we are called – coincided completely in the drama of the murder of Jesus. Malice toward the visible brother formed a continuum with the rejection of the unseen God; the judicial murder of the brother was at the same time an attempt to do away with God . . . Still, as Christians we can at times discern in ourselves the dual drives to be rid of God and our enemy. The desire to be rid of God lies behind all of my sinning; the desire to do away with an enemy is the identifiable extreme of what is wrong with me. This means that any manifestation of drive to be rid of a fellow human being – the hostility-hatred-murder-continuum – carries with it inseparably the drive to be rid of God and veers back across the centuries into that crucifixion of the Christ. p. 45.

45. I am indebted to Dr. Robert and Mrs. Blanche Jensen for helping me put the matter in this way. For the pacifist is tempted to condemn the state to the necessity of war but if we do so we but become the other side of the just-war position. Theologically we may not know how God can provide for the possibility of a non-violent state, but neither can we act as if such were not a possibility.

46. Such a position is at least suggested by the bishops in *The Challenge of Peace* as they say,

> Building peace within and among nations is the work of many individuals and institutions; it is the fruit of ideas and decisions taken in the political, cultural, economic, social, military, and legal sectors of life. We believe that the Church, as a community of faith and social institution, has a proper, necessary, and distinctive part to play in the

pursuit of peace. The distinctive contribution of the Church flows from her religious nature and ministry. The Church is called to be, in a unique way, the instrument of God in history. Since peace is one of the signs of that kingdom present in the world, the Church fulfills part of her essential mission by making the peace of the kingdom more visible in our time (21-22).

In a manner similar to some of the criticism I have made, Joseph Komonchak suggests about the Pastoral, some may "wonder why the bishops do not make more of the redemptive role of Christ and the church as an instrument in history of his word and grace. The latter, of course, is not denied, but it certainly does not occupy a major role. If it had, it might have been possible to stress more than is now done the 'already' aspect of Christian faith." "Kingdom, History, and Church," in *Catholics and Nuclear War,* p. 109

47. I am indebted to Rev. David Burrell, Rev. James Burtchael, and John Howard Yoder for reading and criticizing an earlier version of this paper. Sister Carol Descoteaux contributed much to the edition of the manuscript. I owe a special debt of gratitude to Mr. Charles Pinches for his close critique of this manuscript. I only wish I knew how to respond to the many questions he raised. Rev. Philip Rossi, S.J. and Dr. Michael Duffey of Marquette University also helped save me from some obvious errors.

The Pere Marquette Theology Lectures

1969: "The Authority for Authority,"
by Quentin Quesnell
Professor of Theology at
Marquette University

1970: "Mystery and Truth,"
by John Macquarrie
Professor of Theology at
Union Theology Seminary, New York

1971: "Doctrinal Pluralism,"
by Bernard Lonergan, S.J.
Professor of Theology at
Regis College, Ontario

1972: "Infallibility,"
by George A. Lindbeck
Professor of Theology at
Yale University

1973: "Ambiguity in Moral Choice,"
by Richard A. McCormick, S.J.
Professor of Moral Theology at
Bellarmine School of Theology

1974: "Church Membership as a Catholic
and Ecumenical Problem,"
by Avery Dulles, S.J.
Professor of Theology at
Woodstock College

1975: "The Contributions of Theology to
Medical Ethics,"
by James Gustafson
University Professor of Theological Ethics at
University of Chicago

1976: "Religious Values in an Age of Violence,"
by Rabbi Marc Tanenbaum
Director of National Interreligious Affairs
American Jewish Committee, New York City

1977: "Truth Beyond Relativism: Karl Mannheim's
Sociology of Knowledge,"
by Gregory Baum
Professor of Theology and Religious Studies at
St. Michael's College

1978: "A Theology of 'Uncreated Energies' "
by George A. Maloney, S.J.
Professor of Theology
John XXIII Center For Eastern Christian Studies
Fordham University

1980: "Method in Theology: An Organon For Our Time"
by Frederick E. Crowe, S.J.
Research Professor in Theology
Regis College, Toronto

1981: "Catholics in the Promised Land of the Saints"
by James Hennesey, S.J.
Professor of the History of Christianity
Boston College

1982: "Whose Experience Counts in
Theological Reflection?"
by Monika Hellwig
Professor of Theology at Georgetown University

1983: "The Theology and Setting of Discipleship in the
Gospel of Mark"
by John R. Donahue, S.J.
Professor of Theology at Jesuit School of
Theology, Berkeley

1984: "Should War be Eliminated? Philosophical
and Theological Investigations"
by Stanley Hauerwas
Professor of Theology
at Notre Dame University

Uniform format, cover and binding.

Copies of this Lecture and the others in the series
are obtainable from:

Marquette University Press
Marquette University
Milwaukee, Wisconsin 53233, U.S.A.